LOST LETTERS AND OTHER ANIMALS

www.blacklawrence.com

Executive Editor: Diane Goettel

Book and Cover Design: Zoe Norvell

Cover Art: "Biosphere Spill" by Kirsten Rae Simonsen

ISBN: 978-1-62557-831-0

Published 2021 by Black Lawrence Press.

Printed in the United States.

LOST LETTERS AND OTHER ANIMALS

Carrie Bennett

Black Lawrence Press

"In the Dreaming the land was flat. There were no gorges
and no hills, and no rivers. The animals lived in one tribe and
spoke with one tongue, so they could understand one another."
—Max Berry, *Lexicon*

"It was said that [s]he was hunting stillness and that...
[s]he carried an empty box on h[er] back, a box with a single
eye, which ate time."
—B. Caitling, *The Vorrh*

"For someone who didn't know, did it make a difference
whether a person was dead or just very far away?"
—Jenny Erpenbeck, *The End of Days*

Table of Contents

THE GHOST PLANTS: A FABLE

It's time to look for the ghost plants

draw an elaborate map of forest
and field trails thread

through windmills and birch trees

all the flowers have mouths

the lines lead to a small circle
where you will see the ghosts

and a clock that devours its own hands

Planes move across copper clouds

you make objects with your hands

thin strips of paper
folded into a red-winged blackbird

the map covers every room in the house
a letter waits

to be written you won't find

the right words
until the year collapses into a heap of light

In another story you swallow pills like petals

and watch the performers
juggle watches

somewhere onstage your boyfriend
pushes furniture around as you

close your eyes to the sound of wind chimes

you never worry about hunting or
regret a mural of wings

on stage you forget
to record the static

of silence
as though language were a prop

to follow to fly to furrow back to

A wind unwinds the power lines

you count the number of vibrations

echoing from the leaving
morning becomes a dark crater

even a fleck of lint will stop the sun

you study each shadow
for proper spinning and speed

In another story you never leave

there are many years of writing
the wrong words

you pile the letters
like so many lanterns

a warning to this wanting

you try to convince yourself
to swallow away

you make the word
into *ghostmaker* her figure fades

you walk through the city almost forgetting

You dream a door opens its mouth

words spill out like a message
being written into cloud

more years pass

you carry a red stone

you tattoo a map onto your arms
and study the solar system

a burning current of rings and waves

you pack green plums and paper
you bring your white dog

To prepare you memorize the fable of the failed deer

when she was born
her hooves were small as bolts

her throat so weak
she couldn't drink her mother's milk

her eyes were closed for weeks

you're lucky

you have hands
your mouth is strong

In another story you carry a loon and forge your fingerprints

your boyfriend drinks too much
years before he dies

you watch the lake turn
into a frozen field

you worry about what escapes

a spider web a raven
words become their action

probably closer to blur of blue sky

no not sky or light
not like

objects without their faces

Keep walking deeper into the forest

you see deer creatures
with pale flowers growing from antlers

the trees are shaped like bodies

branches bend into curved backs
faces smudged with leaves

you tie red ribbons to your fingers
and crouch close to the ground

then you see the saddest bloom

it remembers a lot
little seahorse without roots

In another story you carry a box in your mouth

inside a bird sings
until a single bulb blooms so bright

it replaces fire and even the sun

then you will know
where words go to die

everything will be both
new and terrible at the same time

ANIMALS IN PRETTY CAGES

1

The body is old and doesn't know what is being done to it. Just as the mind is old [undone: in the process of forgetting] and doesn't know what is being done to it.

2

This body is female and walks through the house humming a song of two tones [note: not a birdsong, not a wordsong] held together with a wave-rhythm [imagine picking up a glass of milk and swallowing it down again and again]. This song is constant and replaces language. The song should not be interpreted as music but monotony [metaphor: a canary pecking at the same piece of lettuce for an entire afternoon].

3

Like anything else, the body becomes angry if pressed or poked
or prodded. Though the original mind [memory-filled: a white
dog dead many years ago] has been replaced with a new mind
[wordless: an arthritic finger pointing to a lake, hands cupping
a face] the body still navigates the room, still knows how to
grasp a doorknob to open the front door.

4

Eventually all objects will lose their function: toothbrush, toilet,
towel, mirror, door handle will all be a stone thrown into an
enormous pile of other stones.

5

[Aside story: Eventually this body will resemble the story of another body that, when given a banana, picked it up, examined it, and neatly placed it back on the table. When given the fruit peeled, again set it on the table. When given little bite-size pieces held them for a moment and put them back. When these pieces were placed in the body's mouth, the mouth, not knowing what to do, opened back up and let the banana fall.]

6

Banana then becomes stone.

7

[Note: There is no moral, no meaning, just the mind losing itself like a child alone in a vast field.]

8

The tongue can still maneuver the mouth like an awkward and thick string, *I love you* still speakable. But this action is more muscle-memory [without meaning: a blue kite flying against a blue sky].

9

Each night the body repeats itself: fold quilt down, crawl under
quilt fully-clothed with eyeglasses and hat, place head on pillow,
keep eyes open, wait, wait, wait, push quilt back, climb out of
bed, walk into living room, sit in recliner, fold hands over lap,
begin humming above tune, wait, wait, wait, walk back into
bedroom and repeat. [Note: some cats will lick until no fur is
left.]

10

[Dear reader, don't descend that mountain so quickly next time,
notice the miniature yellow orchids, how the family of chicka-
dees are trying to tell you something.]

11

Now there are words like *plaque* and *tangles*. It's not the act of forgetting [remember: the dog was forgotten in his metal crate, inside the closed car, for hours, when the late afternoon reached close to 90 degrees, and this not done by the diseased mind] but the misplacement of the commonplace [a key found in a bowl of plums, a license lodged between dinner plates].

12

When, finally, the dog was remembered in the suffocating car, it was almost too late, its heart almost unhinged, its breath a rusty machine, but even then, the dog showed no malice, only wanting air and grass.

13

Think a woman standing alone inside a forest of tall pines.
Think empty wall, open window, the sea a moving canvas.
Think blue, think blank. And in the picture the body holds
a doll and in the memory the mind never loses its way.

14

*Up up, the blue bird, above, yes, at the end of the hall, on the wall,
high and then there, see, the blue, the little wings, it sits on a fence,
way back, yes, yes. Oh my* says the body, *look, look, it's so,* and ges-
tures toward the lake, *it's so, yes, it's doing and very happy.*

15

Change: one day the canary's feathers are the palest of peach, the next a fierce orange-red. Or, more accurately, the change occurs so slowly as to go unnoticed until, suddenly, one day, the mind registers a variance in color, and forever [everything] is changed. As in, there is no going back.

16

What, exactly, has weakened? How many months ago did you last see her? Can she construct sentences? Can she dress herself? Will she let you bathe her?

17

Remember, it can be helpful to print out pictures of everyday items and activities. Showing a picture of a person sitting on a toilet may help trigger the mind into recognition. If not, force can be used to hold the uncooperative body down.

18

[The body forgets how to be a body.]

19

One day the canary stopped singing and it went unnoticed for a long time, until, one night, at the dinner table, you hear the complete silence, the absolute lack of chatter, of trills, its strange and fierce repetitions. [Note: leave a window open so that the canary can hear outside noises—buses pulling away from the curb, cars honking, sparrow-songs. In the wild silence means danger, some predator close and stalking.] There is no way to tell the canary *you are safe no matter what* and so you give it cucumbers and lettuce, leave a small bowl of water at the bottom of its cage so it can take an early morning bath.

20

At a certain point, the cage becomes bigger. Or, more precisely, the cage isn't the point.

21

The first woman diagnosed was Auguste Deter. The man who diagnosed her, Alois Alzheimer, died at the age of 51.

22

Memory-keeper, memory-collector. A woman holding a burning branch. A woman talking to a doll, a blanket wrapped around its small plastic body.

23

What came first: body or mind?

24

She holds your hand in the sun by the pond reflecting the sky and wind and says *I are happy*.

25

Naming is more important now. [A white dog running across a field, wind, the wind moving the dry grass, the water reflecting sun and sky, cloud and tree, unseen birdsong.]

26

No. Naming becomes important when the ability to name is gone.

POSTCARDS FROM
A MEMORY-COLLECTOR

We try to make a different
wild with new rules. Sky

as ground, cloud as lake.
We decide all animals

have their own secrets.
From the balcony I watch

the sidewalk and imagine
an opened mouth underneath.

I wear the day like a bright
bell in my throat.

We live in a house where every animal was once our mother. Paper boats hang in a forest of doorways and the sky an endless sphere of gray feathers. One night a fox barks at us, the tip of its white tail there then gone. Aren't we all quick ghosts trying to settle ourselves into the night? Each tree is its own shining language. You sit on the floor like a new person. There are clocks and a miniature train circles the room. Light shines on the palm of your hand. Such a small square of pink. The heart is like that too. If we are very still and don't speak. If we do this out of love.

I wake to find turquoise
feathers in my mouth.

Under my pillow a butterfly
wing large enough to cover

my face. I'm trying to locate
the place at the base

of my brain. I think I will
find my childhood there.

It is as if nothing happened
or did you die and I never

even knew you?
I wish I had made that cake.

Sometimes I forget
where my hands go.

I learn that trees can be like people but I don't believe it. Later I move plants around, wait for the bus in the cold, write an email, order a pastry. Go into the dining room and watch the canary become nervous when it looks in the mirror. Keep watching how my finger points at you. When I hear I should prepare for a blizzard I turn off the movie and crawl into bed. Tell me something I don't want to hear. The ground glows with sharp glass, strawberries sprout through the snow. How will I stay warm? Not every part of the body needs to be warm.

Try to think of the trips
you still need to take.

Not the mind and its
stupid repetitions. Listen

to the canary sing
its songs like thin stones

thrown into windows.
Blue curtains turn to sky.

Even the trees hold mirrors.
A shadow moves.

Outside a cat throws
a mouse into the air.

Maybe one more drink will help. Your jacket has white fur all over it and I hold cupcakes in my hands. By afternoon we are two brilliantly blue peacocks walking through a summer day. There are clouds above us, a white house overlooks mountains, a dirt road cuts through a pasture. I like the empty swing, how the red-shuttered windows tightly close. I'm not sure I need a photograph, maybe I can just remember each angle of light. Don't we all have our dark moments? I watch the days pass as though I'm at the movies. My heart beats the same as yesterday.

Last night I dreamt
we walked through a museum

and you said *pick the painting
you can't leave without.*

I chose one of a woman
sitting in a field,

her hands clasped
under her knees.

I don't think so much
about meaning anymore.

I am walking in a field of puppets having a conversation with the sun. What do an elbow and finger have in common? Arms are used as tools, hands are butterflies pinned beneath glass. All the names I need to remember and the early mornings scare me. Somewhere a blue cloudless sky, my own little present I wrap in paper covered in bluebirds. See these are the pieces I brought with me, miniature daffodils filling the corners. My hands open like two unblinking eyes or white empty saucers.

How many beginnings
are there? A deer follows

you until you become
the deer and then

you know how it feels
to hide deep in the forest.

Memories won't return
to you like a bush filled

with doorknobs.
Please don't lose yourself

in the woods. Sometimes
what is gone is also dead.

BRAINBOX PORTRAITS

The brainbox is divided from
the body like a photo graphs
an image. Press a flower in
between each hour to preserve
the exact measurement of loss—
the mouth holds the wind like
a light bulb holds light, outside
the throat breath becomes ghost.
The processing begins when the
mind rewinds.

The brainbox counts time like
a mechanical watch. It winds
itself into a nest that holds each
memory inside a bright blue
bell. The mind hunts and hides
the bells, hollows out a hole to
hold. Hours become paper bags
of flickering candles. Each bell
contains a clue for how words
are worn.

The brainbox is worn on the body like a shell. It contains instructions for encoding memories. Inside the body lungs are paperwhites buried beneath a lake, ribs cage a sky of murmuration. The liver is a speckled stone. Ferns grow as veins and the throat is a feather at the end of a pen.

Possible images for the interior of the brainbox: coral, bone-cloud formations, certain bodies of water, starfish, seahorses, all hand-sized shells, lightning, intestines, raw meat, lace, various stages of bark decomposition, any animal fox-like. These images should be double-exposed and appear inside white paper lanterns.

In the first stage the sky
explodes into an enormous
purple web, forests of coral
bloom from the ground. In the
second stage all the rivers flood
and birds grow horns. Thick
sheets of algae cover buildings,
power lines echo cooing sounds.
In the third stage humans forget
how to walk.

The brainbox begins to burrow
deeper into the skin like a snail
or nail. Now the body fills
with sand and a single stone
settles between the brain's two
hemispheres. Giant windmills
grow in forests, all the trees are
ghosts now. The sky is a single
star, an infinite dream of
forgetting like an empty field.

In the fourth stage the brainbox becomes a sun. Humans turn into a tribe of deer and there is only one language. At night the deer shine from the fireflies that live inside their bones. Each day ends with the trees losing their leaves and each day begins with the leaves growing back.

The animals continue evolving
until they wear their words like
pebbles on their tongues. Then
communication becomes an
extinct bird with red feathers.
Now every field is new and the
mind a monstrous movie. Now
gather the clues of small flowers.
Instructions are inside.

In the final stage there are no
maps to memorize, no yesterday,
no little hello, no lake or shore
or hand to hold. There are no
trees, no branches, no leaves
shining sunlight, no returning to,
no well, no wild, no wonderful
hiding place. There is no
windmill or wind or word worry.

THE LOST LETTERS

These letter-fragments were found in the North Woods.
Sections of text are missing from snow thaw, severe
temperature changes, and ice storms. Deer were found
sleeping by the letters.

**

Maybe I am flying

                        needed

                this letter

                    without

comfort. When I go inside the rooms   my

mind
walls I do not recognize

**

              winter light
                  blue sky.
stark angles across
                                 I need
     the animals warm and safe
                           just sit still
you tell me
          the two red petals
the floor last night
             I take the wrong pills
                        then   I
take the right

**

one day I will ruin everything   I
won't care

remember the body

sit and wait

think back to the
moment   the heart begins to lose itself

red tulips
their vase
how to name what isn't there.

**

      not sure   want to return to the same place
but

                         I am
    skating
               When I prepare
winter
      make sure there are no accidents

**

see the white dog
the small kitchen though I forget what color the
walls were painted.

I tell myself to shut up
constant noise in the
background

how the sky
skates in circles

wrong about the body

today

dark windows   words
feel   uncertain

**

not a good idea this correspondence with
                                        Even
the ceiling is dirty

sometimes I need to leave the house

            always and never but

the mind wakes up   finds itself in trouble
        again

**

so many beginnings

night is a blue chair   the body inside
the body tires

fire no longer means anything
                              there
all over the ground.

**

what did you say something is
happening far away
When I opened the
door   many stones
an unwritten letter.   land

kept expanding
lake   sky

inseparable
In my dreams

no doors

**

the small animal howls
am gone too long.

the envelopes carry   stones I choose
carefully

Another time another
person called me

my mind
a constant animal

**

I never meant to document
                    headlights moving past
                                        an
open sign   the night
                        full of lines and circles
            on a page
                        all I wanted   rest
                boiled water for dinner found

a hole big enough for a small body
                        or cold

                        air seeping through

always time is there

one day memory is
                a green blanket

                                I fold

in a drawer

ACKNOWLEDGEMENTS

I would like to thank the journals in which many of these pieces first appeared in earlier versions with different titles: *Caketrain, The Fairy Tale Review, Horse Less Review, jubilat, The Route 7 Review, South Dakota Review, Spittoon,* and *751.* "Animals in Pretty Cages" was originally published as a chapbook by Dancing Girl Press.

Many thanks to Black Lawrence Press's belief in this work and to the Massachusetts Cultural Council's generous support of these poems through an Artist Fellowship.

Special thanks to Amaranth Borsuk, Jessica Bozek, Brigitte Byrd, Cheryl Clark Vermeulen, Nadia Herman Colburn, Rosann Kozlowski, Kevin McLellan, Anna Ross, and Judi Silverman for their friendship, inspiration, and editing generosity. My unwavering gratitude to Ginger Phakos for her constant support and belief in the process of recovery, without which I would not have written these poems. My love to Jeremy who helps me be a poet and to our daughter who kept me good company with these poems even before she was born. In memory of Chris Eschenbach who first introduced me to puppets in Vermont fields and Adeline Carlson who inspired these poems.

Jeremy Blackowicz

Carrie Bennett is a Massachusetts Cultural Council Artist Fellow and author of biography of water, *The Land Is a Painted Thing*, and several chapbooks from dancing girl press. She holds an MFA from the Iowa Writers' Workshop and currently teaches writing at Boston University. She lives in Somerville, MA with her family.